Be Inspired ...

To Love

Be Inspired ...

To Love

Sister Ave Clark, O.P.

—

__In Memory__ of three "gentle men" who lived lives with a gentle, noble spirit of love.

Gerard Clark
Dr. Frederic Gannon, M.D.
Rev. Paul Palmiotto

What did these three good people have in common?

a man with special needs
a fine doctor
a parish priest

They had the nobility of soul to inspire by sharing their faith...sharing their love.

<u>CONTENTS</u>

Chapters

> The chapters in this book will not be titled or given a page number in the contents. The author invites you to open to a page anywhere and ...

<u>be inspired... to love.</u>

<u>DEDICATION</u>

This book is dedicated to:

Sister Fran Gorman, O.P.

Sister Fran Gorman, O.P. is an Amityville Dominican sister. I call her a good friend. More than that she is truly an example of being Jesus love to all people she meets. The best gift she has is tucked inside her wonderful heart ... a compassionate heart.

PROLOGUE

This is Church ...
> ... no walls
> ... no roof
> ... people present to one another

This is Church ...
> ... signs of Hope
> ... perseverance with boundless
> compassion
> ... forgiveness from the heart

This is Church ...
> ... live your prayer
> ... sacrifice your time
> ... give of your presence

This is Church ...
> ... people gathered in everyday
> marketplace of life
> ... comforting one another
> ... sharing Faith

This is Church ...
> ... when we see Christ's love in everyone
> ... when we see Christ's love everywhere
> we go
> ... when we live what we profess

This is Church ... Welcome Home

AUTHOR'S NOTE

It is over a year since the pandemic arrived at the shores of our country. Lives sadly lost leaving comfort interrupted. Daily lives changed. And yet there is a space for creative love to be shared:

Inspire
Be challenged
Weep with / for one another
Arise each day with mercy
Pray more
Have compassionate thoughts
Do not take anyone for granted
See hope as a guiding light
Be a better listener
Have an understanding spirit
Find solitude life-giving
See Christ's gaze in everyone
Love ... everyday
Imagine ... Peace in every human heart

Each one of us can be a small light. The world needs many small lights to brighten the Universe. We can do it by inspiring one another ... to love.

a small light
it glows
it shows a small faithful path
it offers compassionate peace of mind and heart

a small light
loved by God
sent by God
inspired to speak with love's light within ...
we listen
contemplate
pray...with an open contrite heart
that we too can become
a small light ...

a small light that shares what Jesus said ...
Love one another.

I hope this simple book of shared thoughts is just that:

a small light that says... I care!

Today ... is the best time to take a Prayer~Pause

Pause quietly ...
Pray deeply ...
Share faithfully ...

"Be still ... and know that I am God."

words shared by Joan Davenport

What does it mean to "be still "?
What blessings .... give you hope?

We live in a fast-paced and sometimes very noisy world. It is good for the soul and spirit to take time to just "be still". And in the stillness find more of God's love.

Blessings come when we believe that despite any of life's difficult detours God's presence of hope will be fuel for the journey. "I am with you" he says Now that is blessed assurance.

PRAYER: Lord Jesus, thank you for your daily affirmations. Show me in the stillness of my wanderings that you are my guide ... my heart to heart friend of wonderful compassion ... this I will continue to share with wonderful joy. Amen.

"To accept the path of the gospel each day, even though it may cause us problems, that is holiness."

These are the words of Pope Francis

Am I ready to live and share the Beatitudes in my daily life?
Where is the path of "holiness" leading us?

Every day we are provided with moments of being ... being Christ-like. At times this might take great patience, much hope and plenty of faith-filled prayers.

Holiness means having a heart directed to doing good for others. In other words, we are God's messengers of mercy, love and justice for all.

PRAYER: Lord Jesus, show me the path of holiness. Give me the necessary graces to embrace challenges and even the cross. Help me to be filled with the spirit of the blessings of living and sharing the Beatitudes of Love. Amen.

"It helps to be patient ..."

words shared by Joann Laraia

**What does it mean to "be patient"?
How do we encourage patience in others?**

To "be patient" is to wait with calmness of spirit, to never give up and to believe in the Lord's unconditional patience for us. This is truly a wonderful way to inspire others.

They say patience is a virtue that we sow through trials and setbacks. It enables us to slow down our behavior in a fast-paced world. Together we become more peace-filled in all of our daily encounters.

PRAYER: Lord Jesus, thank you for your "forever" patience.   You teach us to be more understanding of others in their struggles. Bless us with a patient heart that loves others back into a life of peace and serenity. Also, Lord, help us to be patient with ourselves. Amen.

"Grace is the free and undeserved gift of God in our life."

words shared by Peg Riconda

What do you do with a gift given freely?
How can "grace" change our life?

Imagine the wonderful gifts of God that are sprinkled freely throughout the Universe. And many of these gifts arrive in our hearts and spirits. Let's share them for the common good. And then grace gives us the courage, faith and goodness to be the gift incarnate in charity, harmony and peace for all. Gather your graces...sprinkle them everywhere you go.

PRAYER: Lord Jesus, you are the bestower of holy gifts. Thank you for all the graces you have given to me to stir into my life...and the life of others. Your grace sustains me in the shadow times of life...your grace received is an "alleluia" moment to celebrate. Amen.

*"You are responsible for the effort,
but not the outcomes ..."*

words shared by Paula Santaro

What does "effort" mean to you?
What gifts does "effort" give to the world?

Effort is simply described as doing your best. Do not measure yourself according to other people's abilities. Effort shows interests and determination right from the beginning of an endeavor. Bless the everyday efforts you put into life ... believe hope, peace, joy and love will eventually bloom.

PRAYER: Lord Jesus, thank you for blessing my humble efforts to share goodness in the world. Show me how to graciously affirm others so they too feel that their struggles and ordinary efforts can make a wonderful difference in the world. Amen.

"Come to me, all who labor and are burdened, and I will give you rest."
(Matthew 12:28)

words shared by Adolfo Quezada

**When you feel weary or troubled who
do you turn to?
How does gentle caring lift up our spirits?**

When we trust in the Lord, we are able to pour out our hearts. The Lord is there as a refuge in times of fear and anguish. What a wonderful comforting thought. Gentleness is a healing strength given and received with a sense of peace. How wonderful to say ... Lord, I praise you in my rising and as the day goes forward. I praise you in my spirit feeling consoled and whole again.

PRAYER: Lord Jesus, I come to you with my heart bruises as I know you are my loving Savior. You are the love that saves. Help me, Lord, to give this consoling love to those in our society who cry out and very often feel unheard. Let me be your voice, O Lord. Let me say ... "Come to me". Amen.

"Hope is my source of strength ..."

words shared by Angela Lewis

Why do we hope?
Where does hope take us?

Hope engages life as it is ... and in how it can be. Hope is a sacred place of believing more. Hope helps us when we are tested, disappointed, hurt or suffering loss.

Hope is there to flame new beginnings, better ways of being. Hope is always creative. Hope helps us to see clearly, choose well and act right.

PRAYER: Lord Jesus, you are the heart of hope. Your gift of hope helps each one of us to re-imagine our world. Let us all hold on to hope by being courageous, compassionate and full of mercy. Thank you for walking with us. Let us see in one another a miracle of hope. Amen.

"Instead of pointing fingers at one another and ridiculing one another ... we should ... raise our hands in prayer to God."

words shared by Ann Gargiulo

**Why do we judge so harshly another
human being?
How does prayer change an attitude?**

It is easier to look outside ourselves and judge another ... rather than to look within and see where we can be better. Harsh words do not create a loving society.

Perhaps if we took our reactions to disappointments and injustices to prayer ... we might find a better way of dealing with differences and find creative ways to accept change. We might also live our prayer by rejecting violence, abuse and harsh words ... these only create a deeper divide. Believe in prayer that changes life in positive and hopeful ways.

PRAYER: Lord Jesus, you taught us to pray. Prayer is a sacred way of creating new, healthy and life-giving attitudes. Prayer is a way of becoming "better". This is what I hope as I pray ... Lord, give me your grace. Amen.

"COME TO ME ..."

These are the words of Jesus

    ... friendly words

    ... neighborly words

    ... challenging and inspiring words

**Why does the Lord call us?
What does Jesus say?**

The Lord calls us to come to him:

        ... to listen better

        ... to understand better

        ... to believe better

      The Lord's call is an invitation to befriend us on life's journey. He says ... "I love you with an everlasting love ... you are my beloved."

      Many times in prayer we ask the Lord to come to us in our sorrows and trials, in our joys and worries. The Lord says ... "I will always be with you ... be not afraid ... I live within you".

PRAYER: Lord Jesus, this is a prayer of gratitude. Thank you for dwelling within me. Let my life be a prayer of friendship with the Lord. Amen.

"Mistakes ... are a fact of life. It is the response to the error that counts."

words shared by Danielle Sondgeroth

**How do you feel when you make a mistake?
What is the best way to respond
to the mistake of others or
to your own?**

Blessed are the mistakes in life that end up teaching us a lot about life. You know what they say, to err is human and to forgive is divine. Mistakes show us our own humanity. They can also reveal how to create a better way of being by our caring or respectful response.

PRAYER: Lord Jesus, you have an all-embracing heart. Show us all how to grow in the grace of acceptance of our own humanity and that of others. Perhaps, Lord, you are showing us that limitations can mold us into better people ... this for sure is the Good News. Amen.

"An act of love, voluntarily taking on oneself of some of the pain of the world, increases the courage and love and hope of all."

These are the words of Dorothy Day

How do we love when we see a need?
What helps us to act with love?

What is the solution to social problems that hold people back from living with more dignity? I dare to say ... love one another. Jesus did!

We have a heart and spirit that can provide for one another ... a place in the heart of one that cares. Most often solutions do not come from money but rather from a love that lifts up and provides dignity for all.

PRAYER: Lord Jesus, show me the way to give my heart a place that bears with each other's faults and burdens...my own included. Let me be encouraged to live the spiritual and corporal works of mercy. Let us all tend to mending the world's needs with compassionate love. Amen.

"Don't be afraid to be vulnerable."

These are the words of
Dr. Frederic Gannon, MD

Why do we fear our vulnerability?
What blessing is found in vulnerability?

To believe... we are always becoming, then we would not fear our own vulnerability (we all have it!!). Stop hiding it, ignoring it or fleeing from it. Take time to be truly human and find in this wonderful discovery that vulnerability has a blessing called resiliency for the human spirit.

A blessing of hope is found in ordinary courage
      ... people attending AA meetings
      ... survivors of abuse daring to speak the truth
      ... embracing loss and tragedy with hearts of faith
      ... extending peace...again and again

PRAYER: Lord Jesus, thank you for my humanity. I am vulnerable, very vulnerable. Perhaps to see our vulnerabilities as blessings is to see the gaze of Jesus' love. Amen.

A Beautiful Soul

from the book by Sister Ave Clark, O.P.
<u>Arthur: Thank You For
Being Jesus' Love</u>

A stained wrinkled shirt
shoelaces untied
buttons buttoned wrong
no socks on in winter
You are a beautiful soul.
You give away a new shirt to someone in
need
You give thanks for your new shoes
(which you said felt heavenly to walk in)
You smiled at your buttons buttoned wrong
(you accept your limitations with such grace)
You were in a hurry to get to the retreat
and forgot to put your socks on.
You are a beautiful soul.
The pastor made the coffee for the retreat
Someone said it was way too strong
Arthur smiled and said
"I'll put more milk in the pastor's good
coffee."
Like Jesus, Arthur, you lived and shared the
way of goodness.
You are a beautiful soul.

Perhaps in reading this poem on
vulnerability you will discover a blessing

"...whatever you do for the least of my brethren... you do it for me..."
(Matthew 25:40)

words shared by
Sister Irene Weiner, O.P.

Who are the least of the brethren?
What gift does Christ give to everyone?

The least are God's loved ones. Seeing Christ's loving presence in all people is at the heart of the Gospel message. There I am. Serve me. Care for me. Feed me. There might be a time in your life that you were among the least. How did you feel when others reached out to you? Remember in serving one another ... we serve Christ-incarnate.

PRAYER: Lord Jesus, what a glorious gift to have a dwelling place within our hearts and spirits for you. Thank you for the mission to be your hands, feet and caring heart to share with others. It will be in giving ... that we will see and receive Jesus in all of your brethren. Amen.

"Kindness isn't so much what you do...
it is who you are"

These are the words of Father Paul Palmiotto

Is kindness about doing?
How do you become kindness?

Kindness is giving ... freely shared. It is a sprinkling of Jesus love in our words, deeds and actions. Kindness heals. It has no fear in it.

Kindness pours its love into the world without being asked. Kindness from the heart needs no applause ... it comes from a sacred place in the very fiber of one's being. It is God's embrace of life shared.

PRAYER: Lord Jesus, when did we see you hungry ... when did we welcome a stranger ... when did we find you ill or imprisoned?

And the Lord says to each one of us...
"in so far as you shared kindness, you did it to me"

Keep becoming kindness.

"Rejoice in hope ... endure in affliction ... persevere in prayer ..."

words shared by Sister Fran Gorman, O.P.

**How does one faithfully share one's humanity
here on earth?
Life's journey takes us to many a crossroad in life
... what grace arrives?**

When we see people joyful and happy it can be contagious. We find ourselves smiling and joining the joy with a smile and perhaps with some laughter of the heart ... it's good for the soul.

Some crosses in life bring change and offer the person experiencing them a time to trust the Lord more and put a heart-filled prayer there that says ... "Here I am Lord". Best prayer ever!

PRAYER: Lord Jesus, you know my standing and my sitting...you know that my life's journey will have a few unexpected detours. Show me that in all of life your love and grace await me everywhere. Help me to rejoice in my daily resurrections that bless my life. Amen.

"It is my pleasure...to help you."

words shared by my good neighbor
Frank Orlando

... helpful words
... concerned words
... compassionate words
... Good Samaritan words

How can we give genuine help?
What gift of being for another changes the world?

Being sincere in offering help alleviates worries and anxiety. When we connect with another person's need and extend an act of kindness, life is better for everyone.

PRAYER: Lord Jesus, you are there for me always. Let me learn from your unconditional love that I too can be for others. Let me be a source of hope and encouragement for everyone I meet. Amen.

"All will be well ..."

words shared by
Dr. Gloria Durka, Ph.D.

**How can we deal with disruptions in life?
Why do we trust?**

The pandemic comes to the world ... everything is interrupted in ways we never thought possible. What lesson can we conceivably learn from social distancing? And yet, this inconvenient time can be a great teacher of resiliency, selflessness and compassion.

All will be well.

We learn to trust when we step out of our own fears, share them, be for one another and believe the Lord is leading us to a new place of fraternal love. Together we will arise and ***all will be well***.

PRAYER: Lord Jesus, you told us quite often that you would always be with us. Help me to cling to those words, hold onto your kindness and stir the graces for renewal. ***All will be well*** as I feel your presence of divine love reflected in the goodness in all my brothers and sisters in the universe. Amen.

"God is Love ... and anyone who lives in love, lives in God."

These are the words of Jesus ...

     ... promising words
     ... joyous words
     ... loving words
     ... connecting words

**What gift does God give to all people?
How do we embrace this wonderful,
grace-filled gift?**

God gives us love ...
        ... to connect
        ... to invite
        ... to include
        ... to befriend

We embrace this love by being a witness of God's friendship with all people ... no walls, no barriers ... just open hearts.

PRAYER: Lord Jesus, you poured love into this world and into my heart. Let me never be stingy with your love. Let my words, deeds and actions reflect the sunlight of your love everywhere I go. Amen.

"A promise is a promise..."

words shared by Hildemarie Ladouceur

What does a "promise" mean?
How do you share the promise of great caring?

Through life many promises are made...and broken. A promise is a special message one conveys to another. A promise usually has a component of peace in it. Think about that.

The great promise comes from the Lord...

"I will love you with an everlasting love ... "

Imagine ... living a promise with **everlasting love**.

PRAYER: Lord Jesus, thank you for showing us the way to love ... a way of keeping promises with peace-filled caring. May my humble promises be ones of connecting your heart of mercy and compassion to everyone I meet. Amen.

"I Have Called You Friends" ...

These are the words of Jesus ...

... comforting words
... affirming words
... caring words
... kind words

What does it mean to be a friend?
Who is my friend?

A friend is loyal, trusting, listening, accepting, understanding and loving.

A friend is every human being ... needing forgiveness, respect and hope.

PRAYER: Lord Jesus, on the way to the cross you revealed your loving ways ... let each one of us choose to live a loving life. Amen.

"... don't get me out of it ...
get me through it ..."

words shared by Jane Liello

**What hardship have you tried to wish away?
What is the best way to handle a difficulty?**

Most of us in life would rather not have to handle situations that bring anxiety or worry. But being human, we will all have these challenging encounters. The best thing is to deal with any inconvenience, sorrow or trying situation with honestly, respect and extra kindness of spirit. We will become better people for this ... you might just say we will grow in nobility of soul.

PRAYER: Lord Jesus, show us the way to live with charity and justice in all of life's encounters especially with those that lay a cross upon us . Give us the necessary graces to also be there for others so that together we become Christ's heart peace for each other. Amen.

"Just Be ..."

words shared by Joanne Fanelli

How does one "just be" with life's questions and decisions?
What can we learn in this space of "being still"?

Life here on earth has many encounters. Some are filled with delight and wonderful happiness while others bring questions of why, what do I do now, I cannot handle this ... so many worries. We fill up our thoughts and days fretting. Perhaps a better way would be is ... to "**just be**". Be in the space, let the questions sit, let the worry sit still. The answer will come, usually in our brave letting go and being open to a new way of being. Perhaps this space is better called God's space with us ... a space of connecting a renewed spirit.

PRAYER: Lord Jesus, you are my best friend. You are an anchor that holds onto the best of me in life. Give me new insights so as to make good decisions for myself and others that are life-giving. Help me to "**just be**" with you in all ways. Amen.

61

"I feel contented here ..."

words shared by my brother
Joe Clark

    ... appreciative words
    ... accepting words
    ... trusting words
    ... thankful words

What does it mean to be content?
How do we handle change?

These words my brother Joe shared were words my mom said to him when at age 95, due to a serious fall, she moved to an assisted living residence. It took some time and probably it was a struggle but mom eventually came to accept her new living space.

Change is not easy especially moving from a home. I think when people feel support and understanding and are cared about they eventually arrive at a space called "being content". Mom sure did. She so enjoyed her two years at the new residence making friends and being a bell ringer in the choir.

PRAYER: Lord Jesus, walk with us through all the changes in life that each one of us must embrace...to grow. Help us to find our home knowing you are always with us. Amen.

"Hold only love...only peace in your heart ..."

These are the words of John Lewis

How does one keep loving...in the face of injustice? Where do you find heart peace?

God created the world with wonderful goodness. We get to choose to be life-giving people. People who have integrity of spirit take the path of sharing justice, mercy, compassion and forgiveness. This is a challenging path. Along the path you will meet people who will inspire you...to get in ***good trouble***. Be a sign of joy and hope no matter what!

Heart Peace ... is a sacred place where God's love dwells. It is a place where we live out our faithfulness of spirit. We learn to inspire and be inspired by the daily and humble efforts to be goodness in ordinary ways.

PRAYER: Lord Jesus, you sow goodness and love into all the threads of our life's journey. Help us to recognize the call to be love to all in all ways. Be our inspiration to open our heart in an abundance of charity...so that all may have life in just and good ways. Amen.

"Without the darkness, we would all be deprived of the candle of faith."

words shared by Kathy Sheridan

**How do you feel when darkness comes?
When you hold the candle of faith...now,
how do you feel?**

Darkness and light are part of life. Some experiences of "darkness" can be quite wearying. And yet in the darkness a great light can be discovered ... the light of faithfulness. To hold the candle of faith is a humble, courageous and holy way of living and becoming part of the Christ-light of love. Hold your candle gently.

PRAYER: Lord Jesus, you are the light of the world. You teach us in all ways, in the dark and in the light of life, that your love is there for us. Let any struggle, hardship or loss not diminish our life but rather draw us closer to your sacred heart. Give us the strength to carry the light in all circumstances in life. Show us the way of great compassion. Amen.

"Learn from me, for I am gentle and humble of heart"

These are the words of Jesus

**What truly is the meaning of humility?
How do we practice humility of spirit?**

People who are truly humble trust in the Lord. They share ordinary gifts in quiet, hidden and humble ways. Greatness is not in worldly power but rather in weaving goodness into the world.

Humility accepts the human condition with graces for the journey. Accept your gifts, talents and inner goodness as instruments of peace for the world.

PRAYER: Lord Jesus, teach me to be humble ... open to the graces of your presence dwelling within me. All that I am and all that I can be ... let it be a blessing of humble service for thee. Amen.

"The glass is half full..."

words shared by Louise Mendenhall

**How do you view life when things go wrong?
What gift does a positive attitude give
to the world?**

Things do go wrong and we get disappointed. How we handle these experiences has a lot to do with one's attitude. One does need to be honest about a difficult situation but one also needs to believe that this difficulty will not describe one's whole life. Rather how one courageously deals with loss and difficulties will define a life.

Being able to be positive, hopeful and affirming of effort is for sure a glass half full...not empty. People who struggle and get up again and again have a gift of wonderful resiliency ... in fact they are able to share their half full glass so others can have life. Life is not about being perfect but rather about having enough resources to be a fine human being. So, lift up your half full glass of compassion ... and smile.

PRAYER: Lord Jesus, you are our guiding light. You have given to each one of us the necessary graces to reflect your compassion in the world. Be there with each one of us as we share our humanity with a joyful attitude. Amen.

*"Who goes slowly... goes healthy...
and goes far..."*

words shared by Mary Morris

Do you take time to slow down and just be?
What is our goal in life?

If you race through life you will miss a lot of beauty, joy and happiness. So often a schedule, a deadline or our own inpatient feelings cause us to make hasty decisions.

Walk gently and slowly into life's encounters and you might just discover some hidden graces. We look at a map for directions, use a GPS in the car and follow the directions for a favorite recipe. How do we set directions for our journey in life? Jesus says love one another. Now, that is a mighty fine way to define our life goal.

PRAYER: Lord Jesus, you have forever patience. Teach me to take a sacred pause and affirm my inner spiritual compass as the best rudder to steer my earthly journey. One day at a time, one step at a time, one heartbeat of being a loving person. Amen.

"I don't know what my path is called ... I'm just walking on it."

words shared by Annie Esposito

Where has the journey of life taken you?
How does your faith guide and encourage you?

Life changes with detours, stop signs and new beginnings ... it provides us with new ways of being and new attitudes. We might just say life is full of God's grace and for that we are forever grateful. Faith can be a handshake of wisdom shared and a heart that says "I care".

PRAYER: Lord Jesus, thank you for being my companion on life's journey ... I sense your presence in all of life's encounters. I deeply appreciate the strength of your love that helps me to rise above the stress of life's surprises. I offer you my love by reaching out to others and saying: "I am with you with God's love". Amen.

"...keep going forward and look for goodness."

words shared by Peg Franco

What does the future hold?
How does one stay positive and hope-filled?

The future is one step ahead of us. It can be a known goal or an unknown one yet to be decided upon. It can give us hope by pouring goodness into the journey and help us to see life as a wonderful adventure of love, joy and peace.

PRAYER: Lord Jesus, you are the light for the journey. Your ways are full of goodness and joy. Teach us to be good dreamers as we create spaces of kindness for everyone we meet. Let us all cherish the light that provides new ways to be your loving presence in this world. Amen.

"all shall be well and all shall be well... and all matter of things shall be well."
(Julian of Norwich)

words shared by Joan Kovacs

**How can we be positive in difficult situations?
How does one communicate good attitudes?**

Everyone has some type of cross to bear. Seeking help or better coping skills ensures a good way of living through a difficulty or loss. We need to believe in the possibilities of the courage of the human spirit. Some people who have suffered great losses in life ... now help others to carry their burdens with comfort and Hope.

PRAYER: Lord Jesus, you are the best friend who tends to the wounds of brokenness in our world. Teach us to be the Good Samaritan of charity and great caring so that others will arise to new life every day. Amen.

*"Love is kind, patient ...
not boastful ..."*
(1 Corinthians 13)

words shared by Monica Callender

**How do you live these words of love?
Who are some people who show us how to love?**

Each day we can take any encounter in life and find ourselves with an opportunity to love with kindness and patience ... not to boast but rather to lift up one another with words and deeds of hope and peace. A world full of people created to do God's work will provide examples of sharing 1 Corinthians 13 ... just look in the mirror and smile at the witness.

PRAYER: Lord Jesus, your name is love forever. I cannot thank you enough for watching over me and providing the graces to be a reflection of your deep love. You show me the better way to speak and act and how to be a witness to your love in my life. I am so blessed to share your name ... *love*. Amen.

"Jesus is my savior, my helper and my friend."

words shared by Nina Siggia.

**How do you describe Jesus in your life?
What does it mean to be filled with bountiful love?**

There are myriad ways for all of us to describe Jesus ... how wonderful to have someone who cares deeply about each one of us. He's always there ... one might just call Jesus friend of the heart ...unconditional love forever.

Bountiful ... with Jesus' love we can dare to live a life of virtue. He is the sacred heart of sharing ... what an example!

PRAYER: Lord Jesus, you are the light of my soul. You are the embrace of charity. You are the welcome of forever hospitality. Thank you for being my savior, helper and my forever friend. Amen.

"The world is enough for everyone's need but not enough for everyone's greed..."

These are the words of people protesting for better wages for everyone...

    ... unsettling words
    ... courageous words
    ... justice words
    ... prophetic words

How do we care for the common good?
What does it mean to speak truth to life?

Let no one be left at the margins of life. Let us include all people in attaining the necessities of life with dignity.

Let us live the Gospel message ... let us serve one another as Jesus has served each one of us ... with justice and peace for all

PRAYER: Lord Jesus, you show us the way...you invite us to be brothers and sisters of compassion for one another. May we each say, *"Here I am Lord, I come to do your will"*. Amen.

"Let us be "a people ..."

These are the words of Pope Francis

What does it mean to be "a people"?
How can we be "a people" in this world?

To be "a people'" means our family of earth is united by human solidarity. This unity is not material or worldly...that is too easy. This unity is born of "closeness to God" in our daily encounters.

What a blessing to be "a people" anointed by the Holy Spirit. We are "a people" with a variety of colors, cultures, beliefs. We are "a people" given dignity by God. Share this blessing. Become this blessing.

Accept one another....as a brother, a sister...one heart united...under God.

PRAYER: Lord Jesus, teach us to be humble and hopeful, to lift each other up ... for you taught us to be "a people" is in serving one another ... to bring dignity and justice to all. Help me be better ... help me be "a people" of closeness to the Lord's way. Amen.

"Therefore, my beloved brothers, be firm, steadfast, always fully devoted to the working of the Lord, knowing that in the Lord your labor is not in vain."
(1Cor. 15:58)

words shared by Ralph Iskaros.

**What does it mean to be devoted?
How are we God's beloved?**

To give with your heart and soul is to be devoted. To offer your day with Jesus by your side is truly to be doing the Lord's work.

God calls us **"Beloved"** ... we are all called to share in his mission ... our life is a mission. Go now in peace ... to love and serve one another.

PRAYER: Lord Jesus, you call us to the path of holiness...show us how to be your beloved disciple of compassion. Help all of us to be courageous in the witness of our faith. Amen.

"Honor your father and mother, that you may have a long life in the land that God has given you."
(Exodus 20:12)

words shared by Renaldo Scott

**What does it mean to honor?
What blessing can we give to those who
gave us life?**

To honor is to love, respect, give care and above all share our heart at all times. Those who birthed us and those who gave life to us in many ways deserve our quiet dignity and great kindnesses. We are all called to bless one another with a quality of life that says ...

I love you.

PRAYER: Lord Jesus, you were born in humble surroundings but with great, tender love. This is for sure the wonderful mystery of life that unfolds daily in our caring for one another. Let us be the tender caregivers of Jesus love and mercy. Amen.

"I just need a little more time ..."

words shared by Rosalie Dougherty

Do you value the gift of "time"?
Are you mindful of how you use and share time?

Time is a gift ... it is the breath of our life here on earth. What a holy opportunity to be able to share some quiet time with the Lord ... hands folded in prayerful time.

Be mindful that the very essence of time is to be aware of the sacred moments given to us here on earth...to share peace, hope and concern for one another. This is holy time. God will give us a little more ... just for the asking.

PRAYER: Lord Jesus, thank you for the time to befriend others ... to be a sign of joy and hope. Help me to share my time creatively with a heart that says it's a wonderful time ... to love. Amen.

"The love that we have received empowers us to love others..."

words shared by Sister Alice Byrnes, O.P.

How do you receive ... a gift, a compliment, a suggestion?
How have you been empowered to reach out in brave and life-giving ways?

It is wonderful to give ... but it is also a grace to receive joyously and to appreciate what the giver has bestowed on us. Very often a suggestion to be better is a holy opportunity to receive with an open heart.

When we receive kindness, forgiveness and friendship ... it just stirs the soul to do likewise. Let's all give and receive ... and transform the world from greedy and selfish ways to gracious and kind-hearted ways.

PRAYER: Lord Jesus, you give so abundantly of your love to each of us ... help us to be a giver of joy and a receiver with gratitude. Help us to spread this gracious way of living and being with everyone we meet. Amen.

"I am a firm believer that there is no place where God is not"
(Maya Angelou)

words shared by my brother
Joe Clark

Where is God?
How does faith perform ordinary miracles?

We learned a long time ago that God was everywhere. Perhaps in our difficulties and trials we grew in thanksgiving especially for the healing and comforting presence of God ... always there. Our faith can be the beam of joy and hope in this world ... that is a wonderful miracle.

PRAYER: Lord Jesus, you are the very breath of life reborn, restored and renewed. Your presence is a blessing for all of us here on earth. What a gift to till the soil of your love and graces ... thank you Lord for being everywhere. Amen.

"My grace is sufficient for you..."
(2 Cor. 12:9)

words shared by
Sister Anthony Therese Roncallo, O.P.

How does God's grace help us?
Can we share God's graces?

Always remember ... the Lord is your best friend ... ever by your side in good times and in difficult trying times. Grace is a heartbeat away in prayer. When we perform the spiritual and corporal works of mercy we are extending God's loving care to each other. Even in our struggles grace abides in our resiliency to carry the cross.

PRAYER: Lord Jesus, you are a provider of a love that knows no bounds. This is a wonderful gift to share. Help all people to know the Lord is there to embrace us with unconditional love. Let us open our hearts with a hospitality of acceptance and fraternal love. Amen.

"Nothing is perfect...don't ignore difficulties, try to learn from them..."

words shared by JoAnn Gisoldi

How do you feel when things don't go the way you planned?
What lesson have you learned from a difficult time in your life?

A perfect world might just be too boring! Difficulties very often challenge our patience or provide an opportunity to sow our creative spirit. We can become better people when we embrace all of life.

To be able to say I need help or can I help you shows the wonderful connection caring can have for one another...we usually get over or deal better with a difficulty in life when we reach out to someone ... or someone reaches out to us. It is called the bridge of caring.

PRAYER: Lord Jesus, you are there for us all the time. Let us also be there for one another in respectful, life-giving ways. Let our shared words and deeds affirm life for all people. What a positive role model you are, O Lord. Amen.

"Do everything without grumbling or questioning ... and shine as lights in the world as you hold on to the word of the Lord ...".
(Phil. 2:14-16)

words shared by
Sister Carolann Masone O.P.

How do we "not" question so much or grumble too much during times of difficulty? What lifts your spirits?

In the midst of our grumbling and stumbling questions is the heroic decision to live life and to choose a better way ... acceptance, affirmation and a hope shared in simple and humble ways. This will get us through a setback or two.

Very often the example of someone being courageous and accepting of their human condition boosts our morale and gives us an inspiration ... to live the word of God more fully.

PRAYER: Lord Jesus, you sent us examples of your love in one another. Help us to see the courageous side of your spirit by embracing our own human condition with joy and a dignity of spirit. May the light of your mercy and goodness especially surround us in our cross-bearing moments in life. Amen.

.

"Come ... Follow Me."

These are the words of Jesus

Where is the Lord calling us?
How do we respond to the call of love?

God calls us just where we are ... this is truly an invitation to be holy. Look at Oscar Romero and the El Salvador martyrs: Ita, Dorothy, Jean and Maura. The courage to love ... comes from the heart. Look at Arthur, my friend who lived with the disease of schizophrenia. His words of love to us...

"Mercy is in my eyes, my hands and move of all ...
in my heart."
God is calling you ... just where you are.

PRAYER: Lord Jesus, your call to be compassionate with faithful endurance is for sure a blessing for each one of us to be a courageous witness. This call is a holy call to give our heart away so that the world can be a better place...for everyone. Amen.

"I am a fool for God ... but no one else."

words shared by Sister Lucille DeRosa,O.P.

**Why would someone be a "fool ... for God?
What do you value ... how do you live It?**

No one likes to be called a fool ... but in scripture we are told one is a fool who takes up right ways of living no matter what others say ... to forgive 70 times 7 perhaps.

To be so dedicated as to stand up for justice ... to believe God's way is the best way. Let us dare to live our lives with the spirit of God's love guiding our every word, deed and action.

PRAYER: Lord Jesus, you call each one of us to share your love here are earth. Give us the wisdom, the courage, the faith to light our way in all our daily encounters in life. May we each trust that the Lord will give us the necessary graces ... to be a disciple with a holy heart. Amen.

"Do justice ... Love mercy and walk humbly with God."

words shared by Rev. Dr. William J. Barber II

What does it mean to "do justice"?
How do we unite our deeds with mercy
and humility?

Justice is full of compassion and hope. It welcomes everyone to live peacefully together. Let us in our humble humanity let go of our selfish ways and make room for "more love" here on earth.

Why is this not always easy? The question teaches us that the way to live with a humble heart is by being a contrite heart ... creating a world of many colors and many beautiful spirits.

PRAYER: Lord Jesus, may justice reign down from the heavens prophets who teach us the way of the Lord. May we all hear the call to repair and heal the earth by connecting with each other and shining hope wherever we go. Amen.

"Don't be bitter ... be better."

These are the words of
Sister Mary Andrew, O.P.
(my high school English teacher)

**How can illness, loss or tragedy inspire
us to "be better"?
What can we do in trying circumstances?**

We get to choose as difficult as it is ... a path of using whatever has happened ... to be better. Perhaps it is in the daily getting up in spirit that one soars with faith and hope,

The cross ... calls us forth to everyday resurrection moments. Believe that struggles need not diminish our spirits but rather re-engage our lives in creative, loving ways.

Yes ... we can "be better" together in this very human world.

PRAYER: Lord Jesus, you carried your cross with integrity of spirit. Show us Lord how to be an instrument of peace as we embrace our daily struggles, losses and even tragedies. Be with us as we lift up our spirits with courageous peace. Amen.

"Service is Universal"

These are the words of Prince Harry ...

    ...good works
    ...all-embracing words
    ...giving words

What do words mean?
How do we serve?

Words are not just meant to be said ... without meaning.   Words have helping hands and helping hearts.

We serve ...
> ~~when we care for others
> ~~when we go beyond not just to what
> we need ... but to what others need

We serve ...
> ~~when we "Follow Jesus"
> Come....
>> ...be my hands
>> ...be my heart
>> ...be my peace...for all

PRAYER: Lord Jesus, you came to share and give life.   Let each one of us follow your call to be persons of loving service ... ***universal service***.   Amen.

"There are no gifts as precious as the gifts of time and listening."

These are the words of
Sister Joan Chittister, OSB.

What does it mean to share time?
How does one truly listen?

Time is life ... given by our creator. To share time is to share your life. Sharing time means to give breath to life.

Listening is a beautiful gift. It values someone else. To truly listen ... one needs a heart of loving acceptance.

PRAYER: Lord Jesus, thank you for the holy time you have given me to share. It is a blessing and at times a challenge to listen ... so needed. In listening we can be the gift of joy, forgiveness and peace. Teach us to listen in life-giving ways. Amen.

"If their song is to continue ... we must do the singing."
(Compassionate Friends)

words shared by Elaine and Joe Stillwell

How do you heal a broken heart?
How does loss sow seeds of holy compassion?

Love can have a broken heart. Love can heal and remember with joy. Love feels deep loss with tears and mourning. Love crosses the bridge of sorrow to remember with joy.

In memory ... we get up and create a more loving world. Loss provides us with an unassuming grace ... a treasure that directs our very breath so that the world can be a better place.

PRAYER: Lord Jesus, you know suffering and sorrow...lift up our loss. Show us that the way to healing is **to sing ... in memory ... to live with joy**. Let us remember our loved ones as we stir loving meaning into life. Amen.

"Make a difference in a small way."

words shared by my volunteer assistant
Susan Schwemmer

...simple words
...ordinary words
...everyday words
...special words

How does the ordinary action make a difference? What daily actions/deeds call forth life?

Every day can be quite ordinary. However, I would dare to say never boring if we see in each moment of life an opportunity ... to hold a door, help a neighbor or stranger and say "Good Morning" ... that can make all the difference.

We can each make a difference with the grace of knowing we are God's instruments of love and peace, hope and joy in this world. Dare to go out and make a difference!

PRAYER: Lord Jesus, you gift us with life. Let us never take for granted the earth and people everywhere. Thank you, Lord, for the wonderful graces to make a difference by being love here on earth for one another. Amen.

"... let the spirit guide us so we can shine God's love in the world ..."

words shared by Mrs. Theresa Vitalis

How has the spirit touched your life?
What light shines in our world when
we trust more?

We are told that the spirit will bless us and lift up our spirits. What a wonderful promise. Let your spirit soar with goodness and charity galore. When we trust in the loving guidance of the Holy Spirit ... the world will be one of harmony and peace.

PRAYER: Lord Jesus, you blessed us with the gifts of the spirit so that we can be your instruments of peace in the world. Let our hearts shine with your all-embracing love so that all feel our spirits being uplifted to love and serve one another with your tender love. Amen.

"Don't you worry..."

words shared by Father Thomas Ahern

... supportive words
... kind presence words
... spiritual words
... embracing words

When you worry, who do you turn to and why? How do you deal with trials/crosses that cause you to worry?

Usually when we worry, we look to share with someone who will not judge us. We want someone to be there for us, to be a companion on our life's journey.

Best not to push our worries down and ignore them or pretend they are not there. Find someone with whom you can pour your heart out to ... and then find you have the resiliency to deal with the worry in a healthy and life-giving way.

PRAYER: Lord Jesus, you send friends to tell us "*be not afraid, I am always with you*". Thank you for the gift of also becoming a friend for someone in need. Amen.

"Jesus is alive in us and wants us to call upon him with humility of spirit and a heart of hope and faith ..."

words shared by Gertrude Combie

What does it mean to live with humility?
How do we share our hearts of hope and faith?

To be humble is to remember all that we have and all that we are comes from our Creator's goodness ... then we get to share it. When we share mercy and compassion, comfort and forgiveness ... the morning sun of God's love rises within us. Keep your heart set on God's ways and your faith will bring hope, healing and justice to all. Amen

PRAYER: Lord Jesus, you have a heart so big. It makes me smile. It also encourages me to give when I might hold back. Thank you, Lord for nudging me to share with humility ... and then to have others smile with joy. Amen.

"...this too shall pass."

words shared by Vito DiBona

**How do we get through good times
or difficult times?
What does it mean to appreciate <u>all of life</u>?**

Celebrating life is a beautiful way of showing appreciation. Treasure these memories of joy and happiness. There are also moments in life that call upon our faith to be lived with great courage and trust in the Lord. All these moments shall pass ... what we do here on earth is recall to mind the grace to live each moment faithfully, learn from it and become a healthy person that integrates all of life's experiences into the very fiber of our beings.

PRAYER: Lord Jesus, you shared the gift of life with all of humanity. Our journey has taken us to some wonderful experiences; it also has taken us to moments of great loss, sorrow or fear. Give us your love and grace Lord...all shall pass. Let us hold your presence forever in our hearts. Amen.

"Wait for the Lord ..."

words shared by
a woman in domestic violence

What does it mean to be patient?
How do you wait with resiliency of spirit?

Being patient means we do not give up. We wait knowing unconditional love will provide strength for the journey.

A small light of hope dwells within a resilient spirit.   It believes a new way of living and being is always possible.

PRAYER: Lord Jesus, you are there in the midst of turmoil and fear. You hold our hearts and lead us to the light. Thank you, Lord, for being there ... I waited and you came. Amen.

"The flower that blooms in adversity is the most rare and beautiful of all."

These are the words of Milan "The Emperor"

**How do you handle adversity?
What helps you to bloom ... despite difficulties
or setbacks?**

Everyone in life, some more than others, will deal with adversity. What one needs to do is to remember that with love our hearts can deal with life's heartaches. Keep the door to your heart open where encouragement, healing and hope will be welcomed.

PRAYER: Lord Jesus, you are the divine shepherd. Guide me, protect me and remind me to bloom with holy courage, perseverance and heart-peace. Amen.

"Take Heart ... Your Sins Are Forgiven."

These are the words of Jesus ...

> ... compassionate words
> ... forgiving words
> ... life-giving words
> ... bold, brave words

How do you forgive?
Why do you forgive?

Forgiveness comes from a heart open to new life.

Forgiveness is healing... it offers gracious compassion.

PRAYER: Lord Jesus, you offered love from the cross. Let us choose to be a healer with hope for all. Amen.

"... nothing will separate us from the love of the Lord ..."
(Romans 8)

words shared by Sister Ave Clark O.P.

**How do we believe in the presence of God's love in the midst of turmoil?
What grace of prayerful courage gives us hope?**

What a promise the Lord gives us...to be the eternal presence of loving concern. Our faith can remain steadfast in the midst of life's storms...prayer will be the enduring garment of courage.

Let us believe together ... that the unconditional grace of Jesus' loving concern will spark the struggles of our prayers with holy courage so they too become the heartbeat of peace and justice, mercy and uncommon love for all people in the world.

PRAYER: Lord Jesus, come to us in our daily, humble and sometimes struggling prayers. Transform and bless us so we can be more of your unconditional love. Teach us to pray with courage and to live with a love that embraces all of humanity with unconditional love and respect. Amen.

YOUR PERSONAL REFLECTION PAGE

This is your page to inspire others to love. Write your favorite quote or saying. Follow it by two questions and a paragraph of reflection. Close with your prayer beginning with Lord Jesus. Thank you for sharing a reflection in this book.

Quote:

Questions:

Reflection:

PRAYER: Lord Jesus......

EPILOGUE

It is over a year since COVID-19 crisis changed everything in the world. All of Heart to Heart Ministry events and programs had to slow down, stop and adapt in new and creative ways. With the help of fine friends, it did just that...adapt.

Facebook Sunshine Chats, Zoom Retreats, Live Streaming in parishes and weekly Prayer Phone Chat Groups were introduced so people had a connection to the holy in their lives. It has been an inspiring time to continue to share faith heart to heart with many people. It has also been a very supportive time...to be for one another.

It truly is a very humble time to realize that it will be with our hearts and spirits that connect people to Jesus' love. We are all called to be the heart...the very heart-beat of God's love to everyone. No one is excluded...all are embraced.

This pandemic crisis has shown that one does not just survive...one can learn to thrive in new and creative ways. These thoughts and quotes hopefully will encourage you to reflect on how prayer and grace are at the heart of faithful living. They are the blessings and gifts that each one of us can share...to bring peace and hope with love to every human heart...in every corner of the Universe.

"I thank God with all my heart....
whenever I think of you."

(Philippians 1:3)

ACKNOWLEDGEMENTS

I would like to acknowledge all the people who shared their favorite saying or quote for this book. I listened carefully as to why they shared a specific saying. I hope in some small way I captured the essence of their sharing.

Thank you to Susan Schwemmer...my wonderful, dedicated assistant and good friend who helped with the final typing and editing of this book. Her encouragement and suggestions added some fine tuning to the layout of this book. Her life of gracious giving is an inspiration to me and many others. Thank you to Eric Schwemmer for all his behind the scenes extra assistance. Thank you also to Susan Pussilano for providing one of her beautiful paintings for my book cover.

I wish to extend my thanks in prayer for all the people who inspired others through this long year of the pandemic with their acts of selfless charity, hope and peace. Very often it is in the quiet, humble and ordinary deeds of kindness that others felt your love...let's keep inspiring each other to be the hands and hearts of Jesus' love

"Be kind...and become a transforming instrument of Jesus' Love."

Sister Ave Clark, O.P.
Heart to Heart Ministry
718-428-2471
Pearlbud7@aol.com
www.h2h.nyc.

*"Only the wings of Love and Compassion
can lift and carry us...."*

Heart to Heart

Inspire....
to sow seeds of...
Peace
Hope
Kindness
Charity

Inspire ...
to sow seeds of....
Truth
Compassion
Faith
Caring

Inspire everyday ...
to sow seeds of....

Love...Heart to Heart

Give Love ... Love to Give

...that's how to "Inspire"

Made in the USA
Monee, IL
14 April 2021